Edward B. Passano

THREE QUARTERS OF A CENTURY plus TEN
1890-1975

WAVERLY PRESS, INC.
THE WILLIAMS & WILKINS CO.
Baltimore • Easton
1975

Foreword

Part I of this history was written as "A Memorandum to Mark the Seventy-Fifth Anniversary of the Origin of the Dual Organization." Ten years have passed and far-reaching changes have taken place within the Company. Part II chronicles the years 1965–1975 and thus brings up-to-date the story which had its beginning 85 years ago.

Part I 1886–1965

Part II 1965–1975

Part I

1886–1965

An acorn, planted in suitable soil,

may become a mighty oak.

A microscopic bit of protoplasm,

planted in a womb, may become a bull elephant.

These are common phenomena

in the animate world.

But who would suppose that a toy,

planted beneath a Christmas tree, could

become a lusty business enterprise?

The Story

Embryo 1886–1890

This is a memorandum of the origin of the Dual Organization. Well, let it be so. The origin could well have been recognized at an early period—the period, for instance, when two school boys set themselves up as "Williams and McEvoy," informal partners in a printing establishment that had its habitat in the attic of 916 McCulloh Street in Baltimore, a home in a respectable residential district.

Or it could have been recognized a date earlier, when some friend or relative of a boy named John Williams gave the lad a toy printing press for a Christmas gift. That could have been in 1886 or even 1885; no one knows.

In any case we may suppose that John was delighted with the trinket, which must have been able to print calling cards and such-like small items. This intrigued the fancy of John's pal, Jim McEvoy (later to be an executive of General Motors), and the boys started playing in earnest—so earnestly that Jim finally persuaded his father to buy him a real working press; hence the Williams and McEvoy partnership, as aforesaid, and the printing establishment in the McEvoy attic. It was a real working establishment, too. The boys continued with their schooling, but must have given no inconsiderable time to the business. They even had a staff to assist them—one man and one boy.

3

It may be reasonably assumed that the business prospered, in its own small way, for somewhere along the passing months John H. Williams found for himself a career; he would be a printer. He bought out young McEvoy (the transaction came to $600.00) and determined to move into the deep waters of competitive business affairs, to see whether or not he could swim.

So now you must imagine the lad perched on an amorphous pile of the paraphernalia of a printing shop, in a room in downtown Baltimore, fresh off the moving-van that had brought him and his belongings there. The year was 1890. A new enterprise had been added to the Baltimore economy. Without was the raw dusk of a fall afternoon. Within, the twilight was relieved by the glow in the boy's breast. He was Caesar and the Rubicon was at his back.

The Infant Years 1890–1904

A great fire devastated most of the business district of Baltimore in February 1904, and caught up the parent company of the Dual Organization in its midst. Employees gathered at the shop as the fire inexorably approached, saved what they could but many of the records succumbed to the march of the flames. What we now know of those first years has been mostly gleaned from the memories of men, in one casual way or another, so that only a hatful of incidents still remains.

There must have been years of expansion because the firm moved three times during the interval, each time forced by the need for larger quarters. Furthermore, complexities must have arisen to make it necessary or convenient to have a corporate existence. We even know the date and style of that first incorporation; it is shown, under the word "Formerly," on the seal of a successor corporation, impressed upon a copy of the by-laws of that successor. It was: "John H. Williams Company Incorporated December 30th 1892." At

4

Remains of Williams & Wilkins building after the fire.

that time Williams was still a minor, without a father or other adult male relative, so that his board of directors and officers all had to be friends.

He survived, but his need for capital to finance his growing business must have been acute. He turned to a friend, Henry B. (Harry) Wilkins, young man about town, skilled in the social graces, just the man for contacts. Harry had some money to invest, and he also interested the brothers Garrett, John W. and Robert, bankers, in investing. Thus came about a new corporate structure and the pomp of a stately name: Williams & Wilkins Company of Baltimore City.

That is how the company title came about. John Williams was to leave the scene soon afterwards; Harry Wilkins departed somewhat later. But the name was fixed.

One episode from the last decade of the old century clung to the memories of many. In Baltimore at that time, the Bibb Stove Company was a firm of considerable size and prestige, and its annual catalog was regarded as a most desirable plum for a printer. John Williams decided to make a try for it. The powers at Bibb said no; they had had the catalog printed in Baltimore before and the city just didn't have the talent to do the work as they wanted it done; the forthcoming catalog would be printed in Buffalo. John Williams pleaded for a chance. Let him have a page of copy, he suggested, and he would at his own expense set it up and print it, to show them what he could do. This sales technique is common today, but perhaps it was a novelty then. Anyhow, John got the job.

Another marker of the last decade of the century was the Company's first publication venture. It was abortive and inconsequential, but possibly prophetic.

The item was called *'Twixt Cupid and Croesus*. It was a tale of a fictional *affaire d'amour* by one Charles Didier. The vehicle chosen was the facsimile reproduction of a presumed correspondence by

6

letters and telegrams. The novelty took fire and thousands of copies were sold. Encouraged by this chance success, two more books by Didier were published but failed to live up to the promise of the first one.

The success of the Didier book seemed important at the time (it started ideas of giving up job printing altogether and forming a Southern Publishing Company), but it was not. Another incident of the last decade of the century seemed routine when it occurred but turned out to have far-reaching effects that have not even yet run their full course.

The new capital brought into the firm by Wilkins and the Garretts made further expansion possible and in 1897 the active partners felt a need for a person to devote his whole time to salesmanship. Harry Wilkins knew the man to fill the niche—one Edward B. Passano, a fraternity brother who had studied engineering at Lehigh University but was not then working at his profession. The panic-year of 1893 had left economic disaster in its wake and a job was hard to find and had a habit of just petering out after it was found. Young Passano found himself selling printing, of a sort, on commission—the printing of flour-barrel heads in two colors.

When Harry Wilkins made his proposal to E. B. Passano, the latter was not greatly impressed. He was not a printer and didn't wish to be; he was an engineer. The pay offered ($75.00 a month) was somewhat less than his commissions. But it gave him a chance to stay in Baltimore, whereas his present connection involved much travel. Also, Wilkins painted a rosy picture. There was a brand-new press—one that could print letterheads and such with an imitation of embossing that couldn't be told from engraving. Passano could specialize on selling the product of this press and make fortunes for all of them.

He took the job. The first thing he found out was that the new press wasn't running, never had run, and no one present knew how to make it run—so he made it run. After Mr. Pillsbury, what was a fractious piece of machinery?

Thus the young man began a life-time career. He was presently to become chief executive officer of the Company; twice he was to save its life; later, he became its sole proprietor. Not only his own fortunes but the fortunes of his family became involved. The second generation is now in charge, the first Passano having died in 1946. His elder son, William M., is president of The Williams & Wilkins Company; the younger, Edward M., is president of Waverly Press; a grandson, William M., Junior, is vice-president for production of Waverly Press; his grand-son-in-law, Samuel G. Macfarlane, is director of administrative services for Williams & Wilkins.* Only two persons not of the Passano family have ever held top executive positions in the Organization: Robert S. Gill, president of Williams & Wilkins 1942–1953, and chairman of the board 1953–1962; and E. F. Williams, President of Williams & Wilkins 1953–1962 and chairman of the board 1963–1965.

Harry Wilkins never was a significant factor in the affairs of the business although for some years he was its chief stockholder. His other contribution was bringing Edward B. Passano into the picture. Shortly after doing so, he married and went to the Sorbonne in Paris for special study at the Faculté des Lettres. He retained, however, his financial interest in the Company. He was abroad when, about the turn of the century, John Williams received a flattering and lucrative offer of a position in New York.

---

* For the record the above listing should be amplified and updated. William M. Passano was President of the Waverly Press from 1946–1963, was President of the Williams & Wilkins Co. from 1963–1970 and Chairman from 1970 to the present. Edward M. Passano was President of the Waverly Press from 1963–1970 at which time William M. Passano, Jr., became President and Chief Executive Officer, the position which he now occupies. Charles O. Reville, Jr., has been President of the Williams & Wilkins Co. since 1970. Samuel G. Macfarlane is now a Vice President of Waverly Press as is E. Magruder Passano, Jr., Howard P. Wampler, Daniel H. Coyne and Charles O. Reville.

Eager to accept this, Williams asked Passano if he could manage the business if he (Williams) came to Baltimore once a week to consult and advise. This arrangement was agreed upon, but when Wilkins heard of it he was highly displeased. He had invested and persuaded the Garretts to invest; placing the business in the hands of a young and inexperienced man was not to be tolerated. He planned at trip to Baltimore to liquidate the business. This could be called The First Harry Wilkins Crisis.

But the trip was delayed for some reason, and by the time Wilkins got to Baltimore the Passano regime had turned the business from red to black. Instead of shutting up shop, the stockholders, on Passano's request, voted a 25% cash assessment to furnish necessary working capital. Williams was unable to meet this. Wilkins agreed to pay it for him if, in return, Williams surrendered his stock to Wilkins. To preserve his handiwork, John H. Williams agreed to this one-sided bargain, and left his lusty infant enterprise to be reared by others.

The records between the date of John Williams' retirement and the date of the Great Baltimore Fire, already alluded to, are completely lost. Even the memories of Mr. Passano and those others of the staff who survived until 1925 or later were hazy about the period. All have now passed on. One of them (W. F. Williams, for many later years superintendent of the plant) did recall that during the helterskelter period immediately following the fire, our first scientific journal was printed, *The Journal of Zoology;* and also that the first work done when the Company finally settled in a new home was the old friend, The Bibb Stove Catalog.

It can, however, be safely assumed that the Company grew and prospered during those three or four years. The indirect evidence is of course the stiff fight that Edward Passano put up to save it after the fire had done its worst. He would hardly have gone through such an ordeal for a sickly business.

So came the Great Baltimore Fire of February 1904. The resultant disruption may be readily imagined. Some book plates were salvaged, but not much more. In several different printing houses scattered about town, presses were borrowed and manned by the Company's own force. A couple of lofts were rented for the installation of typesetting machines. The business office was located at none of these sites. Binding was done in New York and Philadelphia. And the procurement of makeshift quarters and the necessary transportation facilities were being wildly competed for by dozens of other concerns caught in the same holocaust. Add in the purchase of new machinery and the finding of a new location, plus insurance adjustments and arrangements for financing, and . . .

And Mr. Wilkins, far away in Paris, precipitated The Second Harry Wilkins Crisis. As chief stockholder, he ordered Passano to have himself appointed receiver, take the insurance and any other assets to pay off the Garretts, and send the remainder, if any, to him.

E. B. Passano decidedly did not like that solution. But he found difficulty in getting the several interests together. John Garrett was abroad, as Harry Wilkins was. Robert Garrett was on duty in the fire zone as a member of Troop A of the Maryland Cavalry, and Passano finally found him in a stable where he was in temporary residence—with his horse. There the two young men made Company history by agreeing that the business should be kept going. When John Garrett returned the brothers agreed to buy the Wilkins stock with a cash payment and a series of notes, the money to come from the operation of the business. The entire sum totaled $12,503.82, which being paid, made the Garretts owners of the business. Exit Harry Wilkins.

Three years later, by a similar arrangement, Edward B. Passano bought the Garretts' stock and became sole owner.

Once continuation of the business was settled, a new location

10

had top place on the agenda. A decision was made to give up a down-town address, move to the suburbs, and specialize in the printing of scientific material even though this meant the eventual giving up of some $50,000.00 worth of profitable "commercial" business.

The location finally pitched upon was near what had once been the village of Waverly, but in 1904 was within the city limits of Baltimore. An excerpt from the minutes of a meeting of the board of directors, dated March 22, 1904, records the circumstance:

"The question of location was further discussed and Mr. Passano was authorized to employ an architect to prepare the plans and elevations for the new building to be erected . . . by J. P. Brandon, the owner of the lot, on a rental basis of ten per cent of the amount of the investment."

Another excerpt from the minutes, under the date of April 25, 1904, is also of interest:

"Mr. Passano suggested the desirability of adopting a Press name for the Company and [he was] authorized to do so, and his selection of Waverly Press . . . was approved."

This is the first mention of Waverly Press in the records. It was chosen, of course, by reason of the new location, though the Company could hardly have been occupying the premises only a month after the authorization to employ an architect.

A year or two after settling into the new quarters, another brief flurry into publishing occurred—medical publishing at that, which the Company didn't get to in dead earnest for another quarter century. But this venture was, in part at least, under duress.

This was the way of it. J. C. Allred, a traveling salesman in the South for a medical publishing company, encountered the frequent complaint that all the medical books were written by "damnyankees" and his customers didn't like it. He thereupon conceived the establishment of a company that would specialize in books written *by* southerners *for* southerners. Mr. Allred formed the Southern Medi-

11

cal Publishing Company, and turned to the flourishing and success-ful Edward B. Passano for counsel and advice—also a spot of credit for the manufacture of his books.

The new company published three books, and that was that. Allred sold the unbound sheets (to another medical publisher) and gave Williams & Wilkins title to the bound copies to liquidate his indebtedness. How many of the bound copies we sold is not dis-closed by the records.

Now the year is 1908. The Company is well-grown, full of health and vigor. The toy planted under the Christmas tree has become one of the large and influential printing firms in Baltimore. The years of infancy when the business had to be dandled on the knee, coddled and cuddled, and sat up with o' nights, are over. The impetus of new management has carried it through a sturdy adoles-cence. The horizons are about to widen and John J. Abel is about to rise above them.

Dr. Abel's connection with the Company was inspirational, not administrative. He raised our sights and gave us a new vision. He was professor of pharmacology at the Johns Hopkins University School of Medicine. He was the father of American pharmacology. He was of world-wide reputation. He sensed, as doubtless many others did, a serious lack in the development of American science— and did something about it.

He came to Edward B. Passano to solicit his interest in the publishing (as distinct from the printing) of science material. He argued that, while there were sporadic science journals in America, no concern made a special function of serving the science world. Such enterprises existed abroad, notably in Germany, and at least one was needed here. The advance of civilization depended upon research and its importance was becoming more and more fully recognized every day. Nothing would stimulate research more surely than the ready publication of its results.

12

That sounds a bit trite today, but this was more than a half century ago. Edward Passano saw the point. The upshot was that on March 16, 1909, a contract for the publication of *The Journal of Pharmacology and Experimental Therapeutics* was signed, with Dr. Abel as Editor, a position he occupied until his death in 1938. We still print and publish it.

It was the precursor of many another journal of the same category. This time, publishing "took." Williams & Wilkins had found its future.

The Developmental Years 1909–1932

The advent of a publishing venture necessitated the organization of a Publishing Department, a very small one that could not have consisted of more than three persons. For more than a decade the publishing ventures were confined to periodicals. World events stepped in to accelerate matters. The Archduke Francis Ferdinand was assassinated on the streets of Sarajevo and the event touched off the first World War. American scientists who had turned to Europe for publication of their reports were suddenly deprived of that outlet. This made the demand for American science journals imperative. Many had their inception during the decade, and many of these were under the aegis of Williams & Wilkins Company, either as publishing ventures or under printing contracts. One of the earliest was *The Journal of Official Agricultural Chemists*, which was carried for three volumes. *The Journal of Cancer Research*, *The Journal of Bacteriology*, *The Journal of Immunology*, and *Genetics* followed in quick succession in 1916. *The Journal of Dairy Science*, *The Journal of Urology* and *Abstracts of Bacteriology* came on in 1917, *Botanical Abstracts* in 1918, *Soil Science* in 1919.

But there is little point in continuing the catalog of titles. Once the start was made, American science journals proliferated rapidly. The pace today is probably greater than ever before. In 1924 the

The Waverly building as it appeared in 1910.

Company was able to announce that, in fifteen years, it "has assisted in the development, as publishers, of twenty scientific journals, all of which are still being published, sixteen of them by the Company. Of the four remaining, one is still manufactured in the plant. In addition to these, thirty other periodicals or transactions of learned societies are manufactured. For one publication the Company renders a complete business service, and a partial business service for several others. In the course of this experience, twenty-five scientific publications have seen their inception under [this] roof. The Company is also agent for two periodicals published abroad."

The figures would seem small if compared with the record of growth during the fifteen years elapsed since 1950, but for their time they are highly significant. Those were years too when the red ink was freely splashed about on the periodical publishing books of account. Some few 13 periodicals were able to show a profit almost from inception. But overall, going back to the beginning in 1909, it was 1929 before the break-even point was reached for the group as a whole—twenty years, you might say, of faith, hope, and charity.

An important factor in these developmental years was the gradual installation of the principles of scientific shop management as enunciated by Frederick W. Taylor. As early as 1908, Morris L. Cooke was employed to install the system. Cooke was a pupil of Frederick Taylor and, as it happened, a classmate at Lehigh of Edward B. Passano. The result was a near catastrophe. Either the shop was too small, at the time, to absorb the Taylor system, or the changes required were too radical for quick assimilation—probably the latter. An instance: copy, particularly science copy, is not all "straight matter," as a novel is. There may be several sizes of type required, for text, formula, or tabular matter. The several elements in the copy called for differing skills on the part of the compositor or differing capabilities of machines. Under Taylor principles, the obvious procedure was to cut up the copy according to its compo-

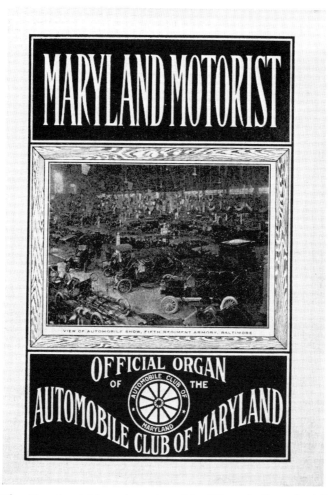

The Maryland Motorist printed by Waverly Press in 1909.

nents, and to have each variety set by a specialist—either hand-compositor or machine. Mr. Cooke had wide powers of discretion and he ordered this to be done. So the copy was set into type with proper efficiency. *But then nobody, nobody at all, knew how to get the several pieces together again in consecutive order.* Everbody connected with the situation—to say it with restraint—was thoroughly annoyed.

The technique has since been mastered. But the experiment caused scientific shop management to be side-tracked for the time being. Later it was introduced bit by bit, with features which were then novel to the industry, although today they are taken for granted. One such feature is a planning department, whose function is to issue detailed instructions to the shop, describing exactly how each job is to be worked; this in contrast to the former custom of depending upon the individual craftsman to make all such decisions. Another is a wage incentive system which rewards the individual worker in proportion to his productivity as measured against standards set by time study. These standard times (and the standard methods on which they were based) are used in estimating job costs, machine loads and production schedules.

Closely attuned to scientific management was the application of engineering principles to the age-old craft of printing. This application was started by F. B. Passano and continued by William M. Passano and Robert H. Roy, both graduates in mechanical engineering of The Johns Hopkins University. Roy, who for many years was Waverly Vice President for Engineering, is now Dean of the Engineering School of The Johns Hopkins University.

The most spectacular accomplishment in the engineering line was the adaptation of the mass production principle of performing each operation in the manufacture of a product to a tolerance sufficiently close that subsequent adjustment is unnecessary. This, known as the "Waverly Precision Program," began with the dimen-

17

sional control of Monotype mats and molds and went through the entire printing process to the maintenance of very fine tolerances in the cylinders and beds of the presses themselves. The entire plant was air-conditioned, for without constant temperature and relative humidity the hygroscopic substances used in printing, such as paper and wood-mounted photo-engravings, will change in size with changes in the moisture content of the atmosphere, and as a consequence no precision is possible. The principle of precision manufacture in the graphic arts industry today is taken for granted, but in 1928, when the Waverly program was launched, it was pioneering and revolutionary.

Another engineering innovation worthy of note was the Roy Type Case, which marked the first real change in the printer's type case since the days when all type was set by hand. The Roy Case was designed for use in the hand-correcting of machine-set composition, and not only speeded the process and reduced the chance of error, but also made it possible, because of its compact nature, to equip each location at which a compositor works with all of the sizes and faces of type carried in the shop.

The structure in Waverly housed the firm for fifteen years. As the end of the period approached the landlord desired a renewal of the lease for another five-year term; but Mr. Passano foresaw that the business would outgrow the premises long before that time expired. He therefore sought to purchase a suitable property in his own name and become the firm's landlord himself. The building he finally decided upon was once the home of the agency that had sold the then as now defunct White Steamer automobile. This was the structure at Mt. Royal and Guilford Avenues, still the central and "home" unit of the Dual Organization. The move was made in 1919. It increased the space available for plant and offices enormously, yet it was not long before the seams began to burst as will presently be disclosed.

18

The publication of journals would probably have led inevitably to the publication of books, but in this case there was a direct connection. In the second volume of *The Journal of Bacteriology* a series of articles by Clark and Lubs appeared. They attracted wide interest and a heavy demand for reprints. It appeared that a book on the subject would find a ready response. Dr. William Mansfield Clark, senior author of the articles alluded to, who later became DeLamar Professor of Physiological Chemistry at the Johns Hopkins University School of Medicine, was persuaded to write the book. Thus *The Determination of Hydrogen Ions* became our first published book (1920) and we claim the honor of counting Dr. Clark among our founding fathers. The book ran through three editions and at least eight printings. When Dr. Clark was asked to do a fourth edition, he threw up his hands hopelessly. The subject had become so ramified, he said, and so much had been written upon it, that even the task of compiling a bibliography was a monumental one.

A portion of this first book, the basic "Color Chart of Indicators," is still in print as a separate pamphlet, and enjoys a steady sale 45 years after its first appearance.

Dr. Clark's book was the forerunner of others, and in 1922 our first catalog appeared. Periodicals were given top billing—the string had increased to fifteen by then —and five books were advertised, including Dr. Clark's and including also a translation from the German of the famous Casimir Funk's *The Vitamines*, original spelling and all.

The first catalog also intimates that we were getting around—around the world, that is. A page is devoted to a "Notice to British Subscribers" (relating to payments, rates of exchange, etc.) with translations into Spanish, French, German and Italian.

Another page in the first catalog solicits manuscripts on twenty different subjects, among which is included (as one subject) "Medi-

WILLIAM M. PASSANO
President Waverly Press 1946–1963.

EDWARD M. PASSANO
President Waverly Press 1963–1970.

DR. JOHN J. ABEL
*First editor of the
Journal of Pharmacology &
Experimental Therapeutics*

DR. WILLIAM MANSFIELD CLARK
*Author of Clark's The Determination
of Hydrogen Ions*

20

cine and Chemistry." An afternote says that manuscripts may be (a) Entirely Scientific, (b) Technical, (c) Popular.

The Publishing Department continued to prosper. The Autumn 1924 catalog listed eighteen journals and fifty books. The feeling arose that continued growth could not be expected if that portion of the business remained as only a department of a printing organization. What we would today call the "image" would be enhanced by separate corporate existence. Mr. Passano determined to make the move and two new corporations came into legal existence in January 1925; one a printer, the other a publisher.

The distinction between printing and publishing is often blurred. Here we have to make the distinction sharp. A printer is not necessarily a publisher—nor is it the nature of a publisher that he be a printer. Either one, however, *may* add to his primary function the function of the other. A publisher may have a printing plant—a printer may have a publishing division.

Printing is a manufacturing process. The printer uses labor, machinery, and raw materials to create a product. Printing is done to order, for customers who pay the printer's bill and use the product for their own purposes. A printer manufactures products that may range from a cheap handbill to an Audubon elephant folio—but he is paid outright for his product. The moment a printer produces a printer piece on his own, on speculation, and offers it for sale to all comers he has stepped into the realm of publishing.

Publishing is an enterprise, a business of buying and selling—of buying (in a sense) an author's manuscript on speculation, of buying the printed book from the printer, and then offering it for sale to the public. A publisher's place of business looks like any other office—desks, people, records, typewriters, a warehouse behind the scenes—and no manufacturing machinery.

The inception of the two new corporations in 1925 was the

Board of Directors of the Dual Organization (1965)

Front row, left to right: Edward M. Passano, President, Waverly Press; Theresa M. Starace, Staff Specialist, Williams & Wilkins; William A. Sager, Vice President for Sales, Waverly Press; Dr. Howard W. Jones, Jr., Associate Professor of Gynecology, Johns Hopkins University School of Medicine; Dick M. Hoover, Vice President and Editor-in-Chief, Williams & Wilkins.

Second row, left to right: John B. Munnikhuysen, Vice President for Research and Development, Waverly Press; Myrtle M. Nichols, Vice President for Personnel, Waverly Press; Charles G. Lord, Partner, Baker, Watts & Co.; Charles O. Reville, Vice President for Sales, Williams & Wilkins; Howard P. Wampler, Vice President for Engineering, and Secretary, Waverly Press; E. F. Williams, Chairman of the Board, Williams & Wilkins.

Back row, left to right: Charles W. Ewing, Vice President Emeritus, Waverly Press; Richard T. Kropf, President, Belding Heminway Company; William M. Passano, President, Williams & Wilkins; Francis C. Lang, Comptroller, Williams & Wilkins; William M. Passano, Jr., Vice President for Manufacture, Waverly Press.

22

obvious inception also of the appellation, "The Dual Organization." Furthermore it raised a nomenclatural problem. "Williams & Wilkins Company" had been the name of the Company since 1893 and it would have been logical to retain this for the parent company and to find a new one for the fledgling. On the other hand "Williams & Wilkins" had been the name under which publication ventures had been undertaken for sixteen years, and it had therefore some value as an identification. Also, "Waverly Press" had been used for some twenty years as the name of the printing plant. The final decision was to call the printing house "Waverly Press, Inc." and the publishing company "The Williams & Wilkins Company."

The relationship between the two is quite simple. Waverly owns all the common stock of Williams & Wilkins and one share of the preferred. The latter has the older name but is subsidiary to the former. All of the common stock of both corporations, and much of the preferred, is held by members of the Passano family. Some forty-six of the employees own varying quantities of preferred shares. The directorates of the two companies interlock. Two non-employees are on the Waverly board: Charles G. Lord, partner in an investment banking house and Richard T. Kropf, president of the Belding Heminway Company of New York. One non-employee is on the Williams & Wilkins board, Dr. Howard W. Jones, Jr., of the Johns Hopkins Hospital staff.

When the move to Mt. Royal and Guilford was made, Edward B. Passano must have gazed to some purpose into his crystal ball. Across the narrow street named Hunter, at the rear of the new location, was a vacant lot in the middle of the block, owned by the city and used for miscellaneous storage. With the possibility of future growth, some time in the next quarter-century, he bought the lot. The quarter-century was over in seven years. In 1926 a four-story structure was built on the northern half of the lot and 12,000 square feet of floor-space were added to the premises. A bridge across Hunter Street connected the two buildings.

23

The Roaring Twenties were on and they continued to roar until the roar suddenly turned into a Ghastly Gasp. On October 29, 1929, the stock market crashed and brought the economy down with it. Aside from the effect shared by all business, the crash may have had an impressive and unforeseen effect on the fortunes of the Dual Organization.

In 1932 there appeared on our doorstep Mr. R. F. West, a director of the London publishers, Baillière, Tindall and Cox. Mr. West was no stranger to us. His company had held, for several years, the British Empire agency for our publications. Mr. West was representing his own company and three other publishers of the United Kingdom. They wished us to purchase William Wood and Company of New York City, established 1805, publisher and distributor of medical books. We gasped, but listened. The country was droning through the great depression. Was this a time for a new undertaking?

But the depression, on the other hand, may have made this acquisition possible. The year 1932 was about its nadir. In more prosperous days, we might not have been given even the chance to make the purchase, or it might have been bid up to a prohibitive price.

Even as it was, the negotiations blew hot and cold over a period of several weeks. The Wood business had come on the market by reason of the death of the last member of the Wood family associated in any way with the enterprise. The dealings were therefore with the executor who was selling the estate. But the active managers also came into the discussions. One of the most valuable of the Wood agency connections was the sale of the Cunningham anatomy books, which were the property of Oxford University Press; these had been handled by Wood in the United States, despite an Oxford branch in New York. Oxford top management thus got into the act, deciding eventually to handle the Cunningham books. Some of our

24

own management group were for the Wood purchase, some against, some indifferent. Edward B. Passano, who would ultimately make the decision, adopted a role almost of neutrality. Whenever negotiations cooled off, the ubiquitous West was on hand to rekindle the fires. The Wood company had been for years American agent for the four companies he represented, and he was eager to have it handed on, intact, to the Dual Organization.

Finally, it came down to this: we should send a representative to New York to try to negotiate a price with the executor. Mr. Passano selected his son William for this delicate task because "you [i.e. William] do not favor this purchase, so you are more likely to get the best possible price. Get the best price you can. If you are satisfied, close the deal. If not, be certain not to close any doors."

The ending was happy. William and the executor came to amicable agreement, and on June 16, 1932, we were in medical book publishing up to our ears.

The Growth Years 1932–1965

Acquisition of the Wood Company immediately added 386 titles to our list. Most of these were of English origin because importation had been a Wood specialty for many years. But there were also many titles of American origin, including quite a few used as textbooks in medical schools. The astonishing vitality of the list is emphasized by the fact that 62 of these titles are still, after a full generation, in new editions in the catalog. Some of the most widely known are May's *Diseases of the Eye*, Cabot's (now Adams') *Physical Diagnosis*, Bailey's *Textbook of Histology*, Stedman's *Medical Dictionary*, Bailey's *Physical Signs in Clinical Surgery*, and Topley and Wilson's *Principles of Bacteriology and Immunity*. One title, not on the present list, went out in a blaze of glory in 1942, when a special printing of 20,000 copies was made for the U.S. Government. This was Tuttle's *Handbook for the Medical Soldier*.

25

Other purchases of medical book "lines" were to follow. In 1943 the medical book department of Little, Brown and Company of Boston was purchased. In 1952, the medical books of Thomas Nelson and Sons of New York were taken over. But these were relatively small transactions.

It was the Wood purchase that seemed to be the fillip that introduced a new range of vision and growth, once a second World War had put an end to the depression. Naturally the purchase had an immediate effect on book sales. By 1940 they had been quadrupled as compared with 1931, and they have gone on from there. The periodicals meantime were sharing the woes of the rest of the nation's business. A high spot had been recorded in 1928, not to be reached again until 1936. In each of three intervening years, the profit on periodicals was less than $100.00.

The depression brought another major factor to the publishing business. This was under duress, so to speak. The sales staff of Waverly Press was, of course, fighting tooth and toenail for elusive business and was much delighted to pick up a major account. The customer was the Mitchell Corporation of Hagerstown, Maryland. The journal was *Current Medical Digest*, edited by Dr. Samuel Wagaman, who was also chief stockholder of the Mitchell Corporation. The *Digest* was to be distributed each month to some 133,000 physicians, without charge, and was to be supported by the sale of space to advertisers.

It was a glowing prospect. But the advertisers did not quite understand their part in the script. The Wagaman capital was insufficient to carry the load far without help. The result was the building up of a printing bill of horrendous proportions. The Organization was faced with the alternatives of swallowing a huge loss or of taking over the *Digest* (Dr. Wagaman was quite ready to allow this) and trying to ride out the storm. Thus the property was transferred to The Williams & Wilkins Company, Mr. Passano

26

Best-selling clinical and research books (1965).

Leading medical school text books (1965).

personally guaranteeing the account. It was a long pull but the *Digest* eventually came to a profitable basis. It is still a going concern.

Someone has said that the greatest problems of the Space Age are closet-space and parking-space. The Dual Organization could safely allege that its space-age problems are concerned with desk-space, machine-space and people-space. In retrospect, time fore-shortens and an evolution that may have taken years seems to have been accomplished in a week or two. Thus it is now, to the retrospective eye, as if the pattern of cramped-for-space, new quarters, plenty-of-room, crowding-up-again, cramped-for-space was not only continual but perennial—happened every year, that is.

Depression or not, it was necessary to build on the other half of the Hunter Street lot a matching four-story structure, which in a few years was followed by a one-story warehouse within a few blocks of the Mount Royal address. A year later, a third floor was added to the Mount Royal building, to be used for Waverly offices, thereby releasing the entire third floor of the Hunter Street structure for Williams & Wilkins offices. These maneuvers were scarcely completed before a new space pinch made itself felt. The factory needed enlargement, more machinery and some place to put it.

It was felt that when a plant grows beyond a certain size, much is lost in the personal relationship between management and employees. Communication becomes cumbersome and *esprit de corps* suffers. It was therefore decided to build another printing plant at some distance from Baltimore, rather than to expand existing facilities. It was further decided to experiment with the principle of bringing the workshop to the rural worker instead of following the common practice of enticing the agrarian worker to the already overcrowded urban complex. After much soul-searching, a five acre plot of ground was purchased at Easton, an attractive small town on Maryland's Eastern Shore about 60 miles from Baltimore.

Some time in the mid-'fifties the City of Baltimore gave notice

29

Waverly Press, Baltimore building purchased from the
White Motor Co. in 1919.

Original unit of the Easton plant built in 1949.

30

that it intended to exercise its right of eminent domain to purchase the warehouse property on Guilford Avenue. This was to make way for a cross-town expressway, then on the drawing boards. (It still is, by the way, only on the drawing boards.)

The result was the construction of a building at 428 East Preston Street, only a stone's throw from Mount Royal Avenue, which contains many long-needed features such as appropriate offices for the publishing business, a two-car railroad siding, off-street loading and unloading facilities for over-the-road tractor trailers, 28,000 square feet of warehouse space, and a parking deck on the roof capable of accommodating 200 employees' automobiles. This structure was occupied in October 1958, and was designed for a 10 year expansion. However, in seven years the publishing force has grown from 75 to 125, and the old cramped-for-space cycle is off on another run around the track.

The most recent building project was an adjunct to the Hunter Street building, which is known as 1310 Guilford Avenue. It was designed, not to increase the Baltimore printing force, but rather to modernize our big city plant. This building makes possible such present-day musts as facilities for interviewing and testing prospective employees, off-street loading and unloading of highway trucks, a lunchroom, an area for research and development where new processes may be proven before being put into production, the automatic baling of waste paper, and the straight-line production of periodicals through the binding and mailing operations.

One might suppose that an organization spread over four locations would encounter some rather trying difficulties in communications. Actually, it isn't so. In the Baltimore area any extension telephone may call any other, precisely as if they were all under one roof. Direct wires from Easton make it possible for any extension there to reach any extension in Baltimore, and vice versa. Telephonic communication is possible with the truck which travels con-

1962 addition to Waverly Press, at 1310 Guilford Ave., Baltimore.

Offices of the Williams & Wilkins Company, 428 E. Preston St., Baltimore, built in 1958.

stantly between the two points. A paging system makes it possible to reach those persons whose jobs require them to move about.

Along with new and larger quarters, the Growth Years have seen much new equipment added to the manufacturing facilities. From the first, of course, attention had always been given not only to the enlargement of such facilities but to the installation of improvements as they came on the market. By 1958 technological advances in the graphic arts were taking place at such a rate that a Director of Research and Development was added to the staff. His sole function is to keep abreast of new processes and machines as they are created. This is a full-time job, and a necessary one, if the company is to maintain its position of engineering leadership in the industry.

In 1956, Linotype machines were installed to supplement the Monotype output. The Linotype casting cycle is much faster than an operator can set the lines. Tape perforators were developed to run the Linotype automatically. These were installed in 1964, along with a high speed Linotype Electron especially designed for tape operation, a change which has greatly speeded up Linotype production.

Since 1962, Waverly has worked with the Miehle Co. to test a new rotary letterpress designed to use duPont Dycril plates. These consist of an ultra-violet-light-sensitive plastic coating applied to a thin steel plate that can be wrapped around a cylinder. They are large enough to accommodate 16 pages. Thus when a 32-page form is demanded, two Dycril plates take the place of 32 individual plates of pages of type. The new press operates at a maximum speed of 6500 sheets an hour—three times as fast as equivalent flat-bed presses.

A case-bindery department was added to the Easton plant in 1961. Automatic equipment for performing all operations in the forwarding and casing-in of hard-bound books has a capacity of 4000 books per day. Case-making equipment will probably be added in the near future.

The tape-operated Elektron Linotype.

A rotary letter-press designed to use duPont Dycril plates later converted to an offset press.

34

The Lanston Monotype Company, early in 1959, asked Waverly to field-test an entirely new Monotype keyboard and caster, designed to increase the number of characters at the control of the operator. The experiment was carried through to success in three years, resulting in increased capacity and reduced costs in the setting of intricate composition.

A Harris offset press was installed in 1964, two additional in 1965, and certainly more in the future. Also under study is an electronic data-processing computer to handle payroll, accounting, inventory control, and much more, including tape perforation for type-setting equipment from raw, unjustified, unhyphenated tape. Photographic typesetting equipment is under active consideration. The product of this process will be film for producing cold type; this will also be operated by perforated tape.

The formation of two related corporations belongs to this period of growth. The first was the erection of the Passano Foundation in 1943, a non-profit organization fostered and supported by the Williams & Wilkins Company. It is operated by a board of six directors, three of whom are members of the medical profession, and three are officers of the Dual Organization. Among its purposes, as set forth in the charter, is that of making "awards for meritorious achievements in scientific research." Such an award has been made annually since and including 1945. Five of the awardees were later recipients of the Nobel prize.

The other related corporation came into being in 1958 as a result of Baltimore city politics. The City Council passed an ordinance assessing a tax on all advertising sold in the city, both on the advertiser and on the seller of the space. This forced the setting up of "The Williams & Wilkins Sales Corporation," which took up its habitat in the neighboring community of Towson, with the sole function of sales of advertising in journals. The ordinance was shortly declared unconstitutional, but the Sales Corporation was

35

Journals published by The Williams & Wilkins Company (1965).

Journals published by The Williams & Wilkins Company (1965).

continued. It has a separate board of directors, but no employees. The necessary work is performed by employees of the Dual Organization.

It is a bit difficult to measure the growth of the Organization by any statistical comparison. The dollar volume of business is unreliable because of the wide fluctuation in the value of the dollar during the period. Because 65% of the business of Waverly is the printing of journals and more than half of the business of Williams & Wilkins is the publication of journals, the growth in the number of journals has some significance. In 1940 Waverly was printing 80 journals, of which 20 were for Williams & Wilkins; in 1965 the number is 158 of which 39 are for Williams & Wilkins. But this is only a fraction of the whole story. The journals have greatly increased both in circulation and in the number of pages in each volume.

Another possible yardstick is the space occupied by the Organization expressed in square feet. In 1919 that footage was 23,000. The Hunter Street annex added 24,000 to that, and the warehouse on Guilford Avenue added 17,000 in the 'forties. The Easton plant, in several stages, added 40,500 more. The Guilford warehouse was lost in the 'fifties and its place taken by 428 E. Preston Street—38,000 square feet. Finally, 1310 Guilford Avenue brought in 21,500 more. In summary, the increase from 1919 to 1965 was from 23,000 to 147,000 square feet—more than six times as much.

Or the measuring-rod of the number of personnel employed may be significant. The original four personnel of two teen-age owners, one man, and one boy of the 1890's had grown to 125 by 1919, to 150 in 1932, and to nearly 700 in 1965.

Let this narrative close with a neat summation lifted from the pages of Baltimore's *Evening Sun* which in turn quotes from the *Publishers' Weekly:*

> Waverly Press, Inc., complete book manufacturers, and Williams & Wilkins Co., major publishers of medical books and journals, have

always constituted, together, a private organization. Their boards of directors, however, have three members who are not in the business, and the firm's house organ comments, in its current issue, "Our outside directors are largely responsible for the fact that we are shedding small business methods and policies."

The firm's slogan, now, is "to remain privately owned but to behave as though we were publicly owned." Accordingly, they have published for the first time an annual report. The firm, with annual sales of $8,000,000, and 700 people employed, is "one of the very few privately owned manufacturing and marketing companies of substantial size left in Baltimore."

L'Envoi

There it is, then. The Life and Times of the Dual Organization through three quarters of a century. A bridge between two worlds—the stodgy, secure Victorian Era and the kaleidoscopic, swift-moving, perilous days of the Atomic Age—across the havoc of two World Wars and the longest and deepest depression the country has every known.

But it survived. It encountered, of course, fair weather and foul, up-years and down-years. It wobbled a bit at the start and even in later times there were occasional years in which Lady Luck scowled. But, on the whole, the ups outvoted the downs. The growth was not spectacular. The earth remained unshaken. But undeniably the story is one of expansion. It could even be called a story of rags to riches.

To the retrospective eye, looking backward over 75 years, certain turning-points are clearly discernible. Retrospection enjoys the advantage of looking backward. "The past at least is secure," as

Daniel Webster remarked to Senator Hayne. A turning-point is not merely an unusual event—it is an event that changes, in the life of a person or an institution, the direction in which he or it is moving. Often, perhaps usually, it is not recognized even by those most active in the event. This is not surprising. If the steps in the new direction have to be retraced for any reason, then the event was not a turning-point but merely an interruption.

The turning-points in the story of the Dual Organization are six in number. Look at them in chronological order.

The first was the procurement of the job of printing the Bibb Stove catalog. This turned the Company from a small-time job shop into an enterprise with prestige, ready to become a force in Baltimore printing circles and in the general business economy of the city.

The second was the entrance of Edward B. Passano in 1897. This could not possibly have been observed as a turning-point at the time. But it was. Here was the man who was to guide the destinies of the enterprise for nearly fifty years and leave a goodly heritage. Twice he was to save it from extinction. As long as he lived it was he who made the decisions significant to the welfare of the enterprise.

The third was the Great Baltimore Fire of 1904 and the consequent move to Waverly. This was a turning-point, not because it was associated with a spectacular disaster, but because of the decision to specialize in the printing of science material, and eventually that only. That certainly was a new direction.

The fourth was the permanent entry into publishing with the inception of the first science journal in 1909. This was distinctly an entirely new enterprise, an embarkation into seas as unfamiliar as the Atlantic was to Columbus before 1492.

The fifth was the initial publication of a book, in 1920. This was, again, a venture into new territory with hazards peculiarly its own.

Curiously enough we may pass over 1925, the year of the birth of the Dual Organization. It was an event to be sure, but not one that changed the course of direction of the business—it merely verified a change already made.

The sixth was the acquisition of the Wood business in 1932. On that has been built the present structure and size of the business. It gave us, ultimately, a position of leadership not merely in the national but in the international publishing and printing world.

Will there be a seventh turning-point? No one knows. No one, indeed, knows whether or not it is already with us, or even behind us. The retrospective eye for the future has not yet been achieved.

Part II

1965–1975

T HE MOTTO on our corporate emblem

is *Sans Tache*—"without blemish."

If this were a boast, it would be a very

silly one, for the errorless life cannot possibly be.

Sans Tache represents

something for which we strive—

a continual aspiration for the present

and future, not a boasting about the past.

The Seventh Turning Point

The final section in Part I lists the six turning points which have taken place in the life of the business and asks the question "Will there be a seventh turning point?" The question has been answered. The seventh turning point did in fact take place in the spring of 1972 when the common stock of Waverly Press, Inc., was for the first time offered for sale to the general public.

On page 39 of Part I a quotation from the Publishers Weekly says in part "The firm's slogan, now, is 'to remain privately owned but to behave as though we were publicly owned.'" This objective, it turned out, stood us in good stead, for when the time arrived when it seemed to be in the Company's best interest to "go public" we have seven years of experience in behaving like a public company with the result that the change was accomplished with a minimum of the traumatic experience which often accompanies such a transition.

At this time a new slogan was coined which said "We are going public in order to remain privately owned." Stock ownership in substantial quantities was in the hands of fourth generation members of the Passano family. The experience of other family owned companies has shown that lack of a market for stock held by those who are not interested in active participation of the business often results in the sale of the company to a conglomerate. It therefore

WILLIAM M. PASSANO JR.
President Waverly Press 1970 –

46

seemed desirable to create a market for those who might wish to dispose of their stock so that those family members who wished to retain ownership and active participation in the management of the Company would be free to do so.

To accomplish the public offering in a tidy fashion one class of stock, Waverly Press common, was issued. Family members and employees exchanged their shares for Waverly common and second and fourth generation family members offered stock for sale to the public which amounted in 27% of the total stock issued. The family's control of the Company remains unshaken, yet those members wishing to cash in their stock are now able to do so.

April 1972 was a propitious time to make a public offering of Waverly Press common. The issue, which amounted to approximately four million dollars was oversubscribed at the offering price of $27 per share. A few months later the stock market started to decline and this fact, combined with the subsequent lackluster performance of the publishing industry in general, adversely affected the price of Waverly Press common despite the fact that sales and earnings have shown a steady increase year after year. As this is written, Waverly Press common pays an annual dividend of $.80 per share and its market price is in the range of $10 per share.

A Third Generation Passano Now Heads the Company

Operating as a public company brought to light the need to completely overhaul our table of organization. In the eyes of the investing public we are one company and the concept of two separate corporations, one for printing and one for publishing, was no longer realistic or appropriate. The Williams and Wilkins Co. therefore has become our book and journal publishing division. We have nevertheless taken pains to retain the W&W imprint on our publications since it has great goodwill value and is associated worldwide with the finest in biomedical literature.

47

The President and Chief Executive officer of the Waverly Press is William M. Passano, Jr. Bill at the age of 46 is the third generation of the Passano family to head the Company which currently employs some 900 persons and enjoys annual sales in excess of 20 million dollars. The other officers as well as the members of the Board of Directors are pictured on the following page. It is worthy of note that eight members of the Board are not in the employ of the Company but rather bring us a rich and varied experience in lines of endeavor which are quite separate from printing and publishing. Without question we have the strongest and most effective Board of Directors in the history of the Company.

Changes in Our Product Line

Interesting changes in the product which we publish have taken place in the past decade. Although we are primarily a printed media publisher, we have adapted to the market demands for new formats and now offer our periodicals in printed and microfilm editions. We have also been successful in publishing audio-visual aids designed to meet particular educational requirements as well as small audio-visual programs developed from our major book offerings.

Medical books remain our standard bearer with emphasis placed on publishing primary and ancillary textbooks and quality specialty books for the clinician. Our editorial staff has grown to accommodate the development of book lines for nursing and the undergraduate areas of psychology, mathematics and the biological sciences. Additionally, we can point with pride to some very well received titles for the specialists within the allied health sciences, particularly physical therapists, speech pathologists, and audiologists.

Our marketing organization has grown to include a large field force for the sale and acquisition of new titles, specialists in direct mail advertising, marketing research and the sale of rights to profes-

48

Officers and Directors 1975

Front row left to right: Richard T. Kropf, President, Belding Heminway Company; Dr. Howard W. Jones, Jr., Professor, Department of Gynecology and Obstetrics, Johns Hopkins University, School of Medicine; William M. Passano, Jr., President, Waverly Press, Inc.; Samuel G. Macfarlane, Vice President, Finance, Waverly Press, Inc.; Edward M. Passano; Dr. J. Roger Porter, Professor and Chairman, Department of Microbiology, The University of Iowa.

Middle row: Pearl C. Brackett, Assistant Superintendent, Baltimore City Public Schools; Daniel H. Coyne, Vice President and President, Publishers Services Division, Waverly Press, Inc.; Barbara J. Bonnell, Director of Information, Charles Center and Inner Harbor Projects; Francis C. Lang, Secretary and Treasurer, Waverly Press, Inc.; David J. Callard, Partner, Alex Brown & Sons.

Back row: E. Magruder Passano, Jr., Vice President and Assistant Treasurer, Waverly Press, Inc.; Arthur W. Machen, Jr., Partner, Venable, Baetjer and Howard and Counsel for the Company; Howard D. Wampler, Vice President and Chief Engineer, Waverly Press, Inc.; William M. Passano; Charles O. Reville, Jr., Vice President, Waverly Press, Inc. and President, The Williams & Wilkins Co. *Missing from the picture:* Semmes G. Walsh, Partner, Baker Watts and Company.

sional bookclubs and reprint houses. Additionally, our book and periodical sales have been organized under the product management concept.

Our Overseas Sales Grow Substantially

The sale of our publications overseas has grown tremendously in the past ten years, with the result that of the total number of our books sold in 1973, 31% were sold outside the U.S. This is considerably higher than the industry average and is something of which we are intensely proud. Our books are distributed in a variety of ways—using the distribution method we have found best suited for the area we are trying to reach.

In Canada and Australia, we have exclusive sales representation. These firms maintain stock of all our books and perform all the publishing functions that we ourselves would do if we had regional offices, e.g., direct mail, journal advertising, exhibits at meetings, college travel.

In Asia, the thrust of our activities is in arranging for co-editions of our books or for exclusive distribution of individual title. At present, published either in Japan or India (and in some cases simultaneously in both countries), are 35 Asian Editions of our books, with another 36 titles being distributed on an exclusive basis. Supplementing the co-edition program, we maintain standing orders for major bookstores throughout Asia, as well as mailing lists of all medical bookstores, medical, dental and veterinary schools, and libraries with a holding of medical publications.

Continental Europe and Great Britain represent the largest market for the original editions of our books. Bookstores receive supplies of our publications within a few days from our stock deposit at Weesp (just outside Amsterdam). Our new publications are brought to the attention of booksellers and instructors by an agency which represents us and a few other medical publishers.

50

An exciting venture for us in 1973 was the publication of International Student Editions of our major textbooks. These are stocked in Beirut and are distributed throughout the Middle East and parts of Africa by a firm which also travels on our behalf in these areas. Our growth in that market in recent years has been especially gratifying.

Latin America, while geographically close, does not represent a tremendous market for English language books. We do have stock in the major cities as well as maintaining standing orders with major stores throughout the area, and we continue to promote to stores, schools and libraries.

Although English continues to be the language of medicine throughout the world, there is still much interest in translation rights to our books. Some 100 titles have been translated into one or more foreign languages. Langman's *Medical Embryology* has been translated into eight languages, the most for any single book, followed by Novak, Jones & Jones: Novak's *Textbook of Gynecology*, which has been translated into five languages.

A Unique Concept

Our Publishers Services Division makes available to others all of the services which we ourselves perform in transforming an author's manuscript into a book or journal placed in the hands of the reader. This is a unique concept and enables those who wish to publish to do so without establishing an organization of their own. We know of no other company which offers to perform for others any or all of the combined functions of printer and publisher.

A listing of services quite naturally begins with the production of the printed product, and here we have layout and design closely followed by redaction of the manuscript. This latter function includes correction of spelling, punctuation, capitalization, abbreviation, faulty syntax and inconsistent style. We also do proofreading,

51

The computer transforms unjustified keyboard input to hyphen-ated and properly justified lines. The result is stored on a disk like the one shown being inserted into the computer. The visual terminal shown in the left of the picture edits and updates the material stored on the disk to incorporate authors corrections.

An editing terminal on which new copy can be set either justified or unjustified or corrections can be made in existing copy.

checking of references and compiling of indexes. Next follows complete bookmaking facilities, including composition, presswork, binding, wrapping, mailing and warehousing.

In the case of journals we promote the sale of subscriptions, maintain a subscription mailing list and do subscription renewal billing, collecting and accounting. We store back volumes and handle reprints ordered by authors and by commercial organizations. We have a large force which promotes the sale of advertising, and in this connection we perform the functions of production billing and collecting.

The Secretary of a society is sometimes inundated with the duties of his office. Dues must be collected and accounted for. Correspondence of a routine sort relating thereto must be answered. A newsletter may have to be produced and mailed. The Publishers Services Division handles these details through its Managerial Service Department.

Many societies hold annual meetings in various cities throughout the land. We stand ready to take care of the almost innumerable details incident to such meetings—rooms for meetings, hotel accommodations, banquet arrangements, registration details and what have you. Frequently there are scientific exhibits or commercial exhibits, or both, in connection with the annual meeting. The details here are also numerous and the demands exacting. We are prepared to take care of them. The Publishers Services Division is proving to be the fastest-growing segment of the Company.

Advances in Technology

During the past decade technological changes have taken place in the graphic arts at a rate which is completely without precedent and they have had a profound effect on the printing process of the Waverly Press. In the beginning we used the Monotype system of composition and flatbed letterpress for printing. Later Linotype was

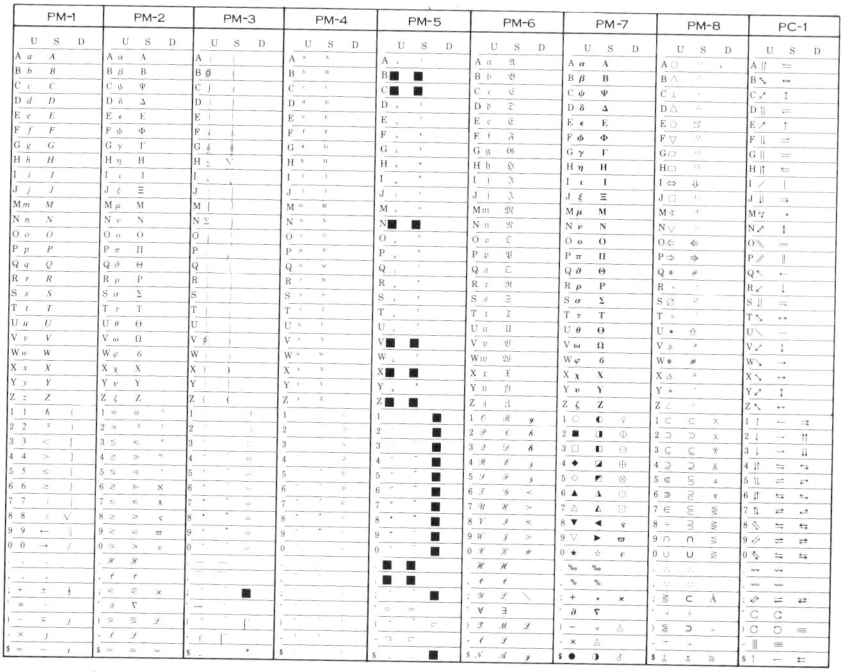
PM-1
PM-2
PM-3
PM-4
PM-5
PM-6
PM-7
PM-8
PC-1
U S D

The characters available on the VIP for composing mathematical and chemical material.

V-I-P

The VIP contains 1728 characters which can be produced in 20 different type sizes. This gives it a capacity 135 times that of the Monotype system which it replaces and makes it invaluable for scientific and technical composition.

added, as were two-color presses, but still the printing process which we employed was in principle similar to that used by Gutenberg. The past several years have seen great changes. Composition is now largely a photographic process controlled by a computer program with the latest equipment acquisition having an output of 80 lines per minute, twice as fast as our first phototypesetting machine. Electronic devices, such as scanners, provide tape for operating the phototypesetter by optical character recognition of typed material, while VDTs (Video Display Terminals) project onto television-like screens the contents of input punched tapes for ease in their updating and/or correction. The computer program to create made-up pages as camera-ready copy from typed manuscript without keyboarding is available now in certain areas of our industry where the composition is relatively simple and straightforward. It will be developed for use with our more complicated type of work in the near future. Camera equipment has become automated and the making of negatives of text pages requires only the placing of new camera copy on a feedboard and the movement of that board to a vertical position. Film is automatically reeled from a roll out to proper length, positioned accurately, exposed, punched for register, and transferred to a processor. Here it is developed, washed, fixed, washed, dried and delivered ready for use—all without human contact except for the initial setting of the camera and the replenishment of film and required chemicals.

Presswork is performed on rotary offset presses, some of the larger ones having roll feeders that utilize stock in roll form and cut it into the desired length at the time of printing. Some of the presses give double output by printing both sides of the sheet on one pass through the press. The binding of periodicals, and even some books, has changed from sewing or stitching to adhesive binding, with an increase in output and a reduction in cost. Hand-fed operations have become automated, and the newest adhesive binder has

Stripping tables where page negatives are imposed into forms from which offset printing plates are made.

On the automatic camera film is developed, fixed, washed, dried and delivered ready for use.

A perfecting press on which 77 inch sheets are printed on both sides at the rate of 7000 sheets per hour.

The bindery fast line on which books are gathered, adhesive bound, covered and trimmed in one continuous operation.

almost twice the speed of operation of our older one. Speed is the order of the day for most processes, and although operating costs have increased with inflation, the cost of the printed work has been held in check by the greatly increased capacity of today's graphic arts equipment. Hot metal and letterpress still have their uses, but fully 75% of our work today is done by cold type and offset. We continue to print a great many specialty journals of modest circulation, but long pressruns are in the ascendancy and the press is geared to handle them rapidly and efficiently.

The Protection of Copyright

No history of the past ten years would be complete without mention of the fight which the Company has waged in an attempt to protect the scientific periodicals against copyright infringement by photocopying. In the early 1960s when the use of the Xerox machine first became widespread, it was obvious that scientific periodicals were in a particularly vulnerable position insofar as copyright infringement was concerned. It was easy to understand that an individual who could obtain from a library a photocopy of the scientific articles in which he had an interest would be less likely to subscribe to the journals in which the articles were published. It was equally easy to see that a library which could serve its patrons' requests for photocopies by obtaining them from another library through the interlibrary loan complex would be less likely to subscribe itself to the journals containing the articles. Consequently, uncontrolled and uncompensated for photocopying posed a threat to the scientific press which could easily do it irreparable damage. We had no desire to curtail photocopying. We considered it an effective and desirable way in which to disseminate scientific knowledge. But we felt very strongly that those who used the scientific journals by photocopying them should share in their support rather than leave the entire burden on the shoulders of the subscribers and, to a limited extent, the advertisers.

58

Unfortunately we were unable to interest the library industry in working to develop a fair and equitable solution to the problem, and with great reluctance we decided to bring a lawsuit and put it up to the courts to decide the equities in the situation.

The suit was filed in February 1968 against the National Library of Medicine (NLM) and the Library of the National Institutes of Health (NIH). These government libraries were selected because they represented two large but quite different photocopying corporations. The NLM is a library's library and is at the apex of the interlibrary loan complex. Another library connected with a medical school or a pharmaceutical manufacturer is free to obtain photocopies of articles from NLM when it does not subscribe to the journals itself. The NIH library, on the other hand, supplies its large research staff with the articles they need by subscribing to one, or at the most, two copies of the journals which contain them.

Almost four years to the day after the suit was filed, the Trial Judge of the Court of Claims found for us on every count and ordered the government to pay appropriate damages. We hoped that this would end the litigation. Librarians had told us that they wanted a court ruling to guide them, but when a simple licensing plan was offered to them which required no record keeping or accounting and which averaged only $3.65 per subscription, they turned it down and forthwith appealed the case to the seven judges of the Court of Claims.

The decision on the appeal was handed down a year later, and much to everyone's surprise, it went against us by the narrow margin of 4–3. The minority report written by the chief judge was most critical of the majority decision and labeled it the Dred Scott Decision of copyright.

At this stage many scientific societies and most publishers of books and periodicals contributed to a fund to finance carrying our case to the Supreme Court. We were happy for this help because it showed that virtually the entire publishing industry had come to agree with the soundness of our position.

In May 1974, the Court agreed to hear the case and oral arguments were heard on December 17 of that year. On February 25, 1975, almost seven years exactly from the date on which the case was first filed, the Supreme Court, with Mr. Justice Blackmun abstaining, voted four to four which allowed the decision of the Court of Claims to stand.

We realized all along that our lawsuit could never serve as an end in itself. Rather it could produce the ground rules to be followed until a revised version of the 1909 Copyright Law was finally enacted and perhaps even act as a guide to Congress in drafting new copyright legislation. The Supreme Court, by its action, gave precious little guidance to the Congress but the lawsuit itself and the closeness of the decision has served a tremendously useful purpose. It has brought the libraries and publishers to the bargaining table with the realization that a fair and workable solution to the problem must be found. As this is written progress in this direction is at long last being made.

Waverly Personnel

The history of the Waverly Press as recounted to this point has dealt with such matters as corporate structure, internal organization, products and processes. The most important ingredient of all, however, is people. The people who make up an organization are what determines its effectiveness in performing the functions which it is in business to perform; in short, its success or failure. The success of the Waverly Press over the past 85 years is due very largely to the caliber and dedication of its employees. These attributes show in the quality of our product and the satisfaction of our customers. They are hard to measure objectively and impossible to tabulate. We shall therefore limit our analysis of the work force to a head count

60

and a description of some of the Company's underlying personnel policies.

In 1974 we had a total of 901 employees of which 45% were women and 25% were black. Thirty-eight percent of the employees had been with the Company ten years or longer and as a group represented 7,557 years of skill and experience with an average of 21.6 years per person.

Many years before fair employment practice became a legal requirement, the Waverly Press policy was to hire and promote strictly on the basis of fitness for the job without regard to race, creed, color or sex. Furthermore, equal pay for equal work has long been a Company mandate. We are proud of the fact that the first black journeymen printers in Maryland were trained and employed by Waverly Press.

A principal reason for the high percentage of long-service people on the payroll is the Company's guarantee of job security. In slack times available work is spread among all affected employees rather than giving full time to some and laying off others. When changes in technology wipe out the need for certain jobs, the persons who held the positions that have become obsolete are trained to new jobs. They are never forced out of work. Even in the great depression of 1930, no employee lost his job nor had his pay cut. No other single factor is so responsible for giving Waverly Press the reputation of being "a good place to work."

For 53 years the Waverly Press has been an "open shop" which means the membership in a trade union is neither a necessity for nor a hindrance to employment. Shortly after World War II two printing trade unions attempted to organize the shop, but when an NLRB supervised election was held, the unions lost decisively and no further union activity was encountered until the spring of 1974. At this time the Graphic Arts International Union claimed to represent a majority of the employees in the Easton plant and petitioned

61

the NLRB for an election. We found that communications between the top management of the Waverly Press and the rank and file at Easton had been allowed to deteriorate, and steps were taken to correct this situation. The election scheduled for August 15 was never held, the union having decided to withdraw its petition for an election. The Company was of course gratified by this turn of events and is now taking steps to permanently bridge the communications gap. A system of employee committees which was instituted in 1946 and which proved to be most effective had been discontinued for fear that it might be judged as a bargaining agent. It is now agreed that most of the committees can be reactivated without untoward effect, and they will not only serve as a vehicle for communication, but, more importantly, as a means of improving the management of the Company. We are looking forward to many more years of uninterrupted open shop operation to the very great advantage of employees and management alike.

Waverly's Customers

No history of the Company is complete without reference to the number of organizations which have been our valued customers for so many years. To paraphrase an old saying, "You can judge a company by the customers it keeps," and in the Appendix are listed the scientific and technical societies which have been served by the Waverly Press for a period of ten years or more.

In some cases we publish one or more journals for a scientific society, in some we supply publisher's services including printing, and in others our contribution is printing only. This is truly a prestigious list which contains the leading scientific and technical organizations in America. The length of the unbroken business relationships represented here is indeed remarkable. Many go back to shortly after the turn of the century. In fifteen years from now the Waverly Press will celebrate its 100th anniversary and no doubt

62

this history will again be updated in recognition of that significant milestone. Our proudest possession will be then, as it is now, the "customers that we keep."

In Conclusion

As an appropriate ending to our Company's history we are reprinting in full, on the following two pages, an article which originally appeared in *The Sunday Sun*, Baltimore, Maryland, June 15, 1975.

Passanos of Waverly Press went 'public to stay private' and liked it

By BRADLEY MARTIN

Kinsmen of William M. Passano, Jr., sometimes jokingly compare him to Michael Corleone, heir and successor to Hollywood's "Godfather." Not that there is even a hint of the mobster in the personality or calling of the blond, open-faced Baltimore executive. The comparison comes, rather, from the fact that Mr. Passano in 1971 formally assumed from the preceding generation the leadership of the extended but closely knit family that has controlled Waverly Press, Inc., since 1907.

The comparison must end there, because the printing and medical-scientific publishing firm takes pride in being "an ethical and moral enterprise"—a company whose written statement of corporate philosophy declares: "Although essential to our existence, purely economic pursuits will not be our only objective."

Waverly Press has a record of success over the years in its essential if not single-minded economic pursuits. It has grown from a small print shop purchased and run by the late Edward B. Passano, grandfather of the current president, to an operation that last year had 961 employees in Baltimore and Easton and recorded almost $22 million in sales.

In printing, it has lived through the technological changes that have made a revolution in the industry in the last few years. It has put up new manufacturing buildings and bought the latest equipment without having to borrow money. In publishing, through its Williams & Wilkins Co. division, it has achieved a position near the top of the heap of companies marketing medical and bioscientific books and periodicals in the United States and abroad.

In the last four years, under Bill Passano, Jr., Waverly Press has changed from a privately owned company to one that still is family-controlled but whose shares are publicly traded. In the process it has streamlined its management organization with increased delegation of responsibility to division chiefs and has, in the view of its executives, begun to emphasize those purely economic pursuits at least a bit more than before.

Now Mr. Passano, 46, and his lean, relatively young management team view their job as increasing profits as a percentage of investment while continuing to grow in a planned, orderly fashion. The growth would come through acquisitions of other, similar companies as well as through increased penetration of markets Waverly already serves.

Improving profits is a particularly pressing matter. Figures for 1974 showed a 43.5 per cent decrease in after-tax income from 1973, following

annual increases that had averaged more than 16 per cent for the previous six years. The company blames last year's poor showing largely on cost increases—not only the general inflation in material and energy costs experienced by the economy at large, but also increases associated with lowered productivity in Waverly's printing operations, where division profits last year were less than $6,000.

This lowered productivity is viewed as a temporary problem that was to be expected as the company entered the final phase of its transition to "cold type" reproduction processes—largely photographic processes that are making obsolete the casting of type from metal throughout the printing industry.

Adding to the cost of the changeover is Waverly Press's policy that no employee should lose his livelihood on account of new technology. Retraining and assignment to a new job on a level equal to his old one is the eventual outlook for a conscientious employee whose job has been automated out of existence, according to Bill Passano, Jr. But in the meantime, he says, such employees in many cases are assigned to lower-level jobs—where they are paid the relatively high wages they were getting in their original positions.

William M. Passano, junior and senior, stand beneath a portrait of the elder William's brother, Edward, in the boardroom of the family-controlled Waverly Press.

When Mr. Passano and other Waverly officials talk about the reason for following this policy rather than downgrading or getting rid of the employees with obsolete skills, it comes out as a mixture of a Passano family tradition of looking out for the hired help and a theory that the costs of thus maintaining employee loyalty will be well repaid in dollars saved over the long haul.

Normal attrition is counted upon to reduce somewhat the surplus of high-paid workers. And if Waverly continues to grow at its current rate, Bill Passano, Jr., says, enough high-level jobs like computer operator and pressman will have to be created in the near future to absorb the remaining people who have watched the dwindling of the hot-metal printing work for which they were trained.

Whatever the long-term results,

Waverly's labor policy has, in the company's view, paid one big dividend already. Last year in the Easton plant a Graphic Arts International Union organizing campaign attracted the support of an apparent majority of workers. The election was delayed long enough for company officials to talk to workers individually—reminding them, the officials say, of the advantages of continuing the old style of labor-management relations. After that, most of the union support evaporated and the union called off the election, promising to try again later.

Although the company plans to continue its policy of protecting workers from the adverse effects of new technology, Mr. Passano says, workers who are not doing their jobs properly will not be kept around and even conscientious workers can expect to see

their overtime work cut or eliminated. A new management emphasis on accountability and efficiency, he says, has grown out of the change to public ownership, increased competitiveness in the markets Waverly serves and escalating costs.

Daniel H. Coyne, Waverly vice president in charge of the printing and publishing services division, estimates that it will be the end of this year before the process transition is completed, and that it might take another year after that to develop the kind of efficiency expected for the longer pull.

Robert G. Wood, an analyst for Baker, Watts & Co. who in the past has recommended the Waverly stock to investors interested in long-term growth, considers solution of the productivity problems essential if the stock is to recover from the current price of about 10—representing just half book value—to levels closer to 27, which was the price at the initial public offering in 1972. For 1975 he predicted only "moderate" increases in earnings to "the area of $1.40 to $1.50 a share"—up from 1974's $1.14 but still a distance from 1973's $2.02. Unaudited first-quarter figures showed a slight improvement over the corresponding period in 1974, with earnings up to 33 cents from 30 cents a share.

"In the long term," Mr. Wood said, "the factors that attracted me to the company in the beginning are still there." These factors, he said, include the stability of the specialized medical publications market. An indicator of long-term growth in that market, he said, is that "the number of people trying to get into med schools—and in fact graduating from them—continues to increase faster than the general public. As you see from paying your doctor's bills, they're not hurting.

Charles O. Reville, Jr., the Waverly vice president who heads the Williams & Wilkins division, says competition in the $70 million-a-year United States medical book market has been increasing, with the number of publishers in the field rising in recent years from about 8 to more than 28. Libraries and institutions, he says, are reducing their buying of medical books and periodicals. Thus, "if you intended to be only in the medical publishing business and if you would not drastically increase your per cent of the market share, it would be impossible to aspire to a growth rate of, say, 10 per cent."

As it happens, Waverly aspires not only to keep selling medical books and periodicals, but also to achieve a rate of real growth of 10 per cent a year—and to do so without switching to markets far removed from its experience, expertise and present manufacturing capability. Mr Reville regards as one answer an expansion from the firm's traditional book-publishing emphasis on graduate education into the undergraduate area—including the community colleges with their burgeoning programs in nursing and the "allied health" occupations.

The firm's move to public ownership, and the events resulting from and surrounding it, Mr. Reville says, have resulted in a tightening of standards on what will be accepted for publication. Waverly since 1973 has reduced by more than half the number of books it publishes annually and is trying to concentrate on works that will become the medical-scientific world's version of best-sellers.

Bill Passano, Jr., emphasizes that growth is secondary to improving profits. "I have no aspirations to take and make this company multiply to a $100 million company," he says. On the other hand, "if it doesn't grow, it's gonna shrink."

The evolution of family-controlled companies is a subject of considerable interest to several members of the Passano family. Both second- and third-generation Passanos know of companies that are withering away due to the directions taken by their family managements. It was as the result of some serious thinking about such matters that the family decided to "go public to stay private."

In the 1960's, William M. Passano, Sr., and Edward M. (Ned) Passano, the founder's sons, were in charge but approaching retirement age. The third generation was solidly represented in management. But no one knew whether the fourth and succeeding generations of the clan would be unanimously qualified and eager to continue the tradition.

The elders watched while other family-held printing and publishing companies reached the stage at which one generation passed from the scene, leaving ownership divided among many heirs. They noticed, William, Sr., remembers, that "when that happens, and there's not a market for the stock, the company is a sitting duck to be bought out by a conglomerate."

Selling some of the Waverly stock to the public was decided on as a way to establish a market price for the shares, so individual family members who should wish not to retain their ties to the family firm could readily liquidate their interests without precipitating a family crisis. Going public also would allow reinvestment of some of the family wealth in diversified portfolios.

In a view of Bill Passano, Jr., the 1972 public offering of 25 per cent of the Waverly stock and the accompanying need to meet government requirements for full-fledged audits and detailed reporting of the company's operations, have been as good for the firm as they have for the family. Waverly is a tighter ship today, he says, "because we've had to please others than ourselves."

65

APPENDIX

A roster of the Journals published by
THE WILLIAMS & WILKINS CO.
together with the name of the Society for which they are the
official organ where appropriate

ACTA CYTOLOGICA
International Academy of Cytology

AMERICAN JOURNAL OF PHYSICAL MEDICINE

THE AMERICAN JOURNAL OF SPORTS MEDICINE
*American Orthopaedic Society for Sports Medicine, Canadian
Academy for Sports Medicine, United States SRI Association,
National Ski Patrol System*

CRITICAL CARE MEDICINE
Society of Critical Care Medicine

DRUG METABOLISM AND DISPOSITION
American Society for Pharmacology and Experimental Therapeutics

GASTROENTEROLOGY
American Gastroenterological Association

INVESTIGATIVE UROLOGY

JOURNAL OF THE AMERICAN AUDIOLOGY SOCIETY
American Audiology Society

THE JOURNAL OF CRIMINAL LAW AND CRIMINOLOGY
Northwestern University School of Law

JOURNAL OF HISTOCHEMISTRY & CYTOCHEMISTRY
The Histochemical Society, Inc.

JOURNAL OF IMMUNOLOGY
American Association of Immunologists

JOURNAL OF INVESTIGATIVE DERMATOLOGY

Society for Investigative Dermatology

JOURNAL OF NERVOUS AND MENTAL DISEASE

JOURNAL OF PHARMACOLOGY & EXPERIMENTAL THERAPEUTICS

American Society for Pharmacology and Experimental Therapeutics

THE JOURNAL OF TRAUMA

American Association for the Surgery of Trauma

JOURNAL OF UROLOGY

American Urological Association

LABORATORY INVESTIGATION

International Academy of Pathology—United States–Canadian Division

MEDICINE

OBSTETRICAL AND GYNECOLOGICAL SURVEY

PEDIATRIC RESEARCH

International Pediatric Research Foundation, Inc.

PHARMACOLOGICAL REVIEWS

American Society for Pharmacology and Experimental Therapeutics

PLASTIC & RECONSTRUCTIVE SURGERY

American Society of Plastic and Reconstructive Surgeons, Inc.

SOIL SCIENCE

Rutgers University College of Agriculture

STAIN TECHNOLOGY

Biological Stain Commission

SURVEY OF ANESTHESIOLOGY

TRANSPLANTATION

The Transplantation Society

UROLOGICAL SURVEY

A roster of the scientific and technical associations,
publishers and organizations served by the
WAVERLY PRESS
for unbroken periods varying from 10–65 years.
Under each is listed the journals and books which we produce for them.

Academic Press, Inc.
Archives of Biochemistry and Biophysics
Developmental Biology
Journal of Ultrastructure Research
Molecular Pharmacology
Proceedings of the Society for Experimental
Biology and Medicine
Virology

The Alumni Association of The Johns Hopkins Hospital School of Nursing, Inc.
The Alumni Magazine

The American Association of Teachers of French
The French Review

American Podiatry Association
Journal of the American Podiatry Association

American Physiological Society
American Journal of Physiology
Journal of Applied Physiology
Physiological Reviews
Handbooks of Physiology

American Psychological Association
Journal of Comparative and Physiological
Psychology
Journal of Counseling Psychology
Journal of Educational Psychology
Professional Psychology

The American Society for Aesthetics
Journal of Aesthetics and Art Criticism

The American Society of Biological Chemists, Inc.
The Journal of Biological Chemistry

American Society for Microbiology
Antimicrobial Agents and Chemotherapy
Applied Microbiology
Bacteriological Reviews
Infection and Immunity
International Journal of Systematic Bacteriology
Journal of Bacteriology
Journal of Clinical Microbiology
Journal of Virology

American Society for Testing and Materials
Annual Book of ASTM Standards—48 parts
Numerous related publications

Angiology Research Foundation
Angiology
Lex et Scientia
Vascular Surgery

Association for Computing Machinery
Communications of the Association for Computing Machinery
Computing Surveys
Journal of the Association for Computing
Machinery
Transactions on Mathematical Software

The Association of the Journal of Neuropathology and Experimental Neurology, Inc.
Journal of Neuropathology and Experimental Neurology

Asthma Publication Society
The Journal of Asthma Research

Cancer Research, Inc.
Cancer Research

Center for Environmental and Estuarian Studies of the University of Maryland
Chesapeake Science

69

Children's Hospital National Medical Center
Clinical Proceedings of the Children's Hospital National Medical Center

The College of Physicians of Philadelphia
Transactions and Studies at the College of Physicians of Philadelphia

Elizabeth Licht, Publisher
Physical Medicine Library 15 titles

Federated American Societies for Experimental Biology
The American Journal of Clinical Nutrition

Hospital for Joint Diseases
Bulletin of the Hospital for Joint Diseases

The Institute of Management Sciences
Management Science

The Institute of Mathematical Statistics
Annals of Probability
Annals of Statistics
Institute of Mathematical Statistics Bulletin

The Institute of Navigation
Navigation

The Institute of Professional Accounting, University of Chicago and London School of Economics and Political Science, University of London
Journal of Accounting Research

The Jewish Memorial Hospital
The Jewish Memorial Hospital Bulletin

The Johns Hopkins University School of Hygiene and Public Health
American Journal of Epidemiology

Linguistic Society of America
Language

Los Angeles Society of Neurology and Psychiatry and The Southern California Neurosurgical Society
Bulletin of the Los Angeles Neurological Society

Medical Library Association
Bulletin of the Medical Library Association

The Mt. Sinai Hospital, New York, N.Y.
The Mt. Sinai Journal of Medicine

The Nathan W. Ackerman Family Institute and The Mental Research Institute
Family Process

National Council on Radiation Protection and Measurements
Reports

New York Academy of Dentistry
Annals of Dentistry

Operations Research Society of America
Bulletin of the Operations Research Society of America
Operations Research
Transportation Science

The Rockefeller University Press
The Journal of Cell Biology
The Journal of Experimental Medicine
The Journal of General Physiology

Scott Publishing Co.
Standard Postage Stamp Catalogue, Vols. I, II, III
United States Stamp Catalogue, Specialized

Seismological Society of America
Bulletin of the Seismological Society of America

Sociedad Matematica Mexicana
Boletin de la Sociedad Matematica Mexicana

The Society for Clinical and Experimental Hypnosis
The International Journal of Clinical and Experimental Hypnosis

Society for General Systems Research
Behavioral Science

Society for Industrial and Applied Mathematics
SIAM Journal on Applied Mathematics
SIAM Journal on Computing
SIAM Journal on Control
SIAM Journal on Mathematical Analysis
SIAM Journal on Numerical Analysis
SIAM Review

The Society for Psychophysiological Research
Psychophysiology

The Society for the Scientific Study of Sex
The Journal of Sex Research

The Society for the Study of Aesthetics
Journal of Aesthetics and Art Criticism

Theological Studies, Inc.
Theological Studies

University of Puerto Rico Mayaguez Campus Agricultural Experiment Station
The Journal of Agriculture of the University of Puerto Rico

We are also proud of the customers whom we have added in (comparatively) more recent years and we acknowledge them in the following listing.

Academy of Marketing Science
Journal of Academy of Marketing Science

The American Academy of Periodontology
Journal of Periodontology

American Association of Dental Schools
Journal of Dental Education

The American Association of Neurosurgical Nurses
Neurosurgical Nursing

American Cleft Palate Association
The Cleft Palate Journal

The American College of Foot Surgeons
Journal of Foot Surgery

American Geriatrics Society
Journal of the American Geriatrics Society

American Heart Association
Circulation Research

American Maritime Cases, Inc.
American Maritime Cases

American Medical Women's Association
Journal of the American Medical Women's Association

American Physical Therapy Association
Journal of the American Physical Therapy Association

American Powder Metallurgy Institute
International Journal of Powder Metallurgy

American Society of Plant Physiologists
Plant Physiology

Association of American Medical Colleges
Journal of Medical Education

Biosciences Information Service
Biological Abstracts

College Art Association of America
Art Journal

Council on Foreign Relations, Inc.
Foreign Affairs

Hospital for Special Surgery
Journal of the Hospital for Special Surgery

Institutes of Religion and Health
Religion and Health

International Commission on Radiation Units and Measurements
Reports

Jefferson Law Book Co.
Journal of Law and Education
Journal of Maritime Law and Commerce

Alan R. Liss, Inc.
Journal of Supramolecular Structure
Catheterization and Cardiovascular Diagnosis

Maryland Historical Society
Maryland Historical Magazine

New York State Society of Certified Public Accountants
CPA Journal

Raven Press
Journal of Cyclic Nucleotide Research
Epilepsia

Regional Science Research Institute
Journal of Regional Science

Society for Applied Spectroscopy
Applied Spectroscopy

Society of Colonial Wars in the State of Maryland
Maryland Colonial Warrior

The Society of Quality Technology
Journal of Quality Technology

The Society for the Study of Reproduction
Biology of Reproduction

Society for Technical Communication
Technical Communications

University of Baltimore
University of Baltimore Law Review

The University Press of Hawaii
Philosophy East and West

William Alanson White Psychiatric Foundation
Psychiatry

Yale University
Yale University Publications in Anthropology